Women of the Confederacy

by Barbara A. Somervill

Content Adviser: Lisa Laskin, Ph.D.,
Department of History,
Harvard University

Reading Adviser: Rosemary G. Palmer, Ph.D.,
Department of Literacy, College of Education,
Boise State University

COMPASS POINT BOOKS
MINNEAPOLIS, MINNESOTA

Compass Point Books
3109 West 50th Street, #115
Minneapolis, MN 55410

Visit Compass Point Books on the Internet at *www.compasspointbooks.com*
or e-mail your request to *custserv@compasspointbooks.com*

On the cover: A Southern woman sews a uniform for a Confederate soldier

Photographs ©: The Granger Collection, New York, cover, 19, 21, 23, 24, 36, 38, 41; Prints
Old and Rare, back cover (far left); Library of Congress, back cover, 9, 15, 16, 27, 28, 29, 37;
Bettman/Corbis, 4, 11, 13, 40; North Wind Picture Archives, 5; Stock Montage, Inc., 6; Stock
Montage/Stock Montage/Getty Images, 7; The Museum of Confederacy, Richmond, Va., 18; The
Museum of the Confederacy, Richmond, Va., Photography by Katherine Wetzel, 20; Time Life
Pictures/Mansell/Time Life Pictures/Getty Images, 31; Mary Evans Picture Library, 32;
Corbis, 35.

Editor: Shelly Lyons
Page Production: Noumenon Creative
Photo Researcher: Abbey Fitzgerald
Cartographer: XNR Productions, Inc.
Library Consultant: Kathleen Baxter

Creative Director: Keith Griffin
Editorial Director: Carol Jones
Managing Editor: Catherine Neitge

Library of Congress Cataloging-in-Publication Data
Somervill, Barbara A.
  Women of the Confederacy / by Barbara A. Somervill.
      p. cm.—(We the people)
  Includes bibliographical references and index.
  ISBN-13: 978-0-7565-2033-5 (hardcover)
  ISBN-10: 0-7565-2033-9 (hardcover)
  1. United States—History—Civil War, 1861-1865—Women—Juvenile literature. 2. Women—
Confederate States of America—Juvenile literature. I. Title. II. We the people (Series) (Compass Point
Books)
  E628.S68 2006
  973.7082'0975—dc22   2006003942

TABLE OF CONTENTS

DIXIELAND

Confederate soldiers lined up in their gray, wool uniforms. The officers' silver buttons shone in the bright sunlight. A drummer set the pace, and the men marched off to war. Women and children lined the streets, singing, "Hurrah! Hurrah! For Southern rights, hurrah! Hurrah for the Bonnie Blue Flag that bears a single star."

The women cheered and smiled without understanding what it truly meant to have a war take place in their backyards. Over the next four years—1861 to 1865—they

A military parade marched through the streets as soldiers prepared to go off to war.

Women watched in horror as battles took place near their own homes.

would learn. While the men, young and old, left for the fighting, most Southern women stayed home to deal with enemy soldiers, disease, and the loss of loved ones. They learned to manage farms, care for households, and handle the businesses their husbands and fathers left when they went to war.

What caused the states to go to war against each other? Southerners believed that states had the right to make their own laws. Southerners did not want

Northerners telling them what to do, especially when it came to slavery. The South's economy was based on a plantation system. Plantations, or large farms, usually produced one main crop of cotton, rice, tobacco, or sugarcane. Plantation owners didn't pay their workers; they owned them. Many Northerners wanted to keep the South's system of slavery from spreading. Others, called abolitionists, wanted to end slavery completely throughout the United States.

Southern plantation owners used slave labor to increase profits.

The issue of slavery had been discussed for years, but it came to a head with the presidential election of 1860. People in the South worried that if Abraham Lincoln won the election, he would order that all slaves be freed. Southern plantation owners believed they could not make money without slave labor.

Abraham Lincoln was the 16th president of the United States.

Abraham Lincoln did win the election, and a month later, on December 20, 1860, South Carolina seceded, or withdrew, from the United States. During the coming months, 10 more Southern states followed: Alabama, Arkansas, Florida, Georgia, Louisiana, Mississippi, North Carolina, Tennessee, Texas, and Virginia. The Confederate States of America was formed and Jefferson Davis became its president.

On April 12, 1861, Confederate troops attacked Fort Sumter, in Charleston, South Carolina. Union troops eventually surrendered and the Confederacy had its first victory. The Civil War had begun. Southern men expected the war to end within weeks. Their wives, mothers, and sisters certainly hoped that was true. But they were wrong.

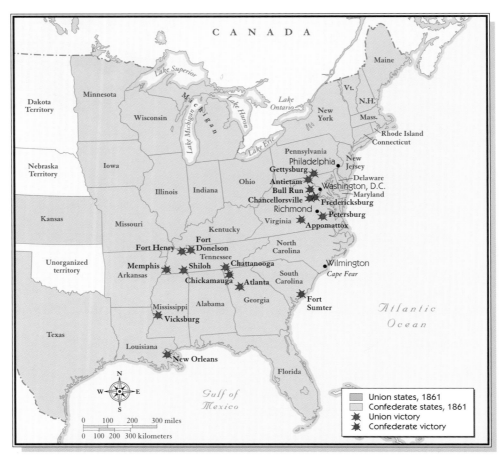

The American Civil War split the United States apart and included many bloody battles.

Fort Sumter, a military fortress in the harbor of Charleston, South Carolina, was occupied by U.S. troops, but the Confederates wanted it for themselves.

The bloody war lasted four long years before Southern soldiers came home, defeated and discouraged.

Southern women had no idea what sacrifices they would make for the war effort. But whether they knit socks for soldiers or charged into battle, they made a difference and set an example of bravery and perseverance.

9

SOLDIERS, SMUGGLERS, SPIES

In the 1800s, a woman's place was in the home, not on the battlefield. Women were believed to be too delicate and weak to survive in rough conditions and face combat. But, not all Confederate women stayed home. Some traveled with the troops and helped cook, do laundry, and tend wounds. Other women cut their hair to disguise themselves and joined up as soldiers. Heroic women hefted rifles on Civil War battlefields, took aim, and fired. Still others became smugglers and spies.

Women disguised as men trained, marched, and lived among their fellow soldiers. They ate the same miserable food. Women suffered wounds from the enemy and injured the enemy in turn. They marched through unbearable summer heat and shivered from cold rain. How did they do it?

Amy Clarke joined General Braxton Bragg's Army of Tennessee. Disguised as a man, she enlisted with her

Soldiers clashed for three days at the Battle of Gettysburg in July 1863.

husband. He died at the Battle of Shiloh, where Amy was wounded. In a later battle, she was wounded again, but this time she was captured by the Union Army. When they discovered she was a woman, they handed her over to officials in the Confederate Army. The Confederates released her from her duties as a soldier. But Clarke returned to

Tennessee, disguised herself again, and rejoined her troops. Texan Robert Hodges Jr. saw Amy and wrote home, "One of the soldiers directed my attention to a youth apparently about seventeen years of age well dressed with a lieutenant's badge on his collar. I remarked that I saw nothing strange. He then told me that the young man was not a man, but a female."

Lucy Matilda Thompson and Loreta Janeta Velazquez also went to war dressed as men. Thompson was a tall woman. She rode, hunted, and shot as well as— or better than—most men. Thompson married in 1861 at 49 years old and wasn't about to let her husband go to war without her. She cut her hair, wore a uniform, and lived as a soldier. Thompson, who was from Georgia, was a successful soldier and survived the war.

Loreta Janeta Velazquez did her soldiering as Lieutenant Harry T. Buford, complete with fake mustache and beard. She proved that women could be excellent soldiers. Velazquez did admit, however, that, "There are some

things which men can do better than women, and digging
[ditches] in frozen ground is
one of them ... nature had
evidently intended me for
a warrior rather than for a
dirt-digger."

Some women bore
arms for the Confederate
cause yet never left home.

The Nancy Harts were
an all-female militia in La
Grange, Georgia. Forty-plus
women became expert marks-

*Loreta Janeta Velazquez
disguised as Harry Buford*

men to protect their town. The group was named for the
Revolutionary War heroine Nancy Hart. They never went
into action because raiders never attacked La Grange.

Shortly after the war began, the Union Navy set up a
blockade of Southern ports. No goods entered or left ports

in cities such as Charleston, Savannah, and New Orleans. The blockade prevented food, cloth, weapons, and medicine from being shipped to the South. Because Southerners desperately needed the supplies, some women began smuggling goods from the North to the South. They sewed smuggled items into their large hoop skirts and petticoats. For example, Belle Edmondson of Tennessee hid quinine, a medicine used to treat malaria, in her skirt hem and safely carried it past Union lines.

Many Southern women made excellent spies, too. Living in Washington, D.C., Confederate spy Rose O'Neal Greenhow entertained Union officers and Northern politicians in her parlor. Greenhow charmed her guests and learned military secrets from them. She sent coded messages to General Pierre G.T. Beauregard about troop movements and plans. Greenhow helped the Confederate general win battles, including the first Battle of Bull Run in 1861. The Union Army caught on to Greenhow and put her under house arrest. She later wrote a book called *My Imprisonment*, in which she told of her experiences as a Confederate spy during the war.

Belle Boyd, called La Belle Rebelle, proved to be a determined spy for the Confederates as well. Union officials arrested her at least six times for spying. Boyd even continued spying while in Washington's Carroll Prison. A friend shot an arrow into her window to tell her how she could pass on information from the prison.

Rose O'Neal Greenhow and her daughter

A note attached to the arrow read, "Procure a large india-rubber ball; open it and place your [message] within it ... then sew it together. ... Then throw the ball ... across the street into the square, and trust to me, I will get it."

Maria Isabella "Belle" Boyd

Some say this plan worked, and Boyd was able to bounce valuable information back and forth from her cell.

Whether hiding needed goods in the hems of their skirts, or passing valuable information in a rubber ball, these Southern women took risks because they believed in the Southern cause. They wanted to do more than sit by and watch as the war took place in front of them.

TENDING THE WOUNDED

When the Civil War began, only men could be nurses. Caring for wounded soldiers was considered too crude for Southern ladies. Often male and female slaves provided nursing services, as well as cleaning and cooking for Confederate hospitals. Many wounded soldiers owed their lives to the care provided by enslaved women.

Throughout the war, the South did not have enough hospitals, doctors, nurses, medicine, or bandages to tend to injured and ill soldiers. Some women set up sickbeds in their parlors and dining rooms. Kate Cumming opened her Mobile, Alabama, home to the wounded soldiers. She wrote, "The men are lying all over the house on their blankets, just as they were brought from the battlefield. They are in the hall, on the gallery, and crowded into very small rooms. ... We have to walk and, when we give the men anything, kneel in blood and water."

Many of the Civil War's bloodiest battles took place

in Virginia. Richmond, the Confederacy's capital city, became a hospital zone. Two major hospitals, both staffed by women, provided needed medical care. Phoebe Pember was a hospital matron at Chimborazo, one of the largest military hospitals at the time. It spread across 40 acres (16 hectares) and could hold more than 3,000 patients.

Pember wrote about her experiences in *A Southern Woman's Story*. She faced shortages of medicines, bandages, and skilled help, yet did not leave her post. She believed her duty prompted her to remain with the sick and wounded, like a general who would not desert his troops in battle.

Another Virginia woman, Sally Louisa

Phoebe Pember's book preserved the history of Chimborazo hospital.

Tompkins, took nursing to a new level. She asked a family friend to donate his Richmond home for the creation of a hospital. She named the hospital Robertson House, for the donor, and opened for business. Many African-American slave women worked as nurses in Tompkins' hospital and saved countless lives. Tompkins and her nurses

Sally Louisa Tompkins founded Robertson House.

had high standards of cleanliness, which saved the lives of many of their patients. In the 1860s, many soldiers did not recover from surgery. They got infections and died, but fewer died in Tompkins' care. Robertson House handled more than 1,300 patients and only 73 soldiers died there.

Some seriously injured Confederate soldiers were treated at Robertson House.

President Jefferson Davis commissioned Tompkins as a captain in the Confederate Army so she could receive rations and a salary to help pay hospital expenses. She kept her hospital open until the war's end.

In many cases, nurses fought against nearly hopeless odds. Twice as many soldiers died of disease than of combat wounds during the Civil War. The major illnesses were diarrhea, typhoid, typhus, malaria, pneumonia, and smallpox. Diseases often took hold of the soldiers before they arrived at hospitals. Many had not bathed in months. They lacked decent food and were exhausted. The soldiers were run-down, and often too weak to survive surgery. Cornelia

Confederate nurses often read to soldiers or helped them write letters to loved ones.

McDonald of Winchester, Virginia, watched the war through her window. "There we sat, all that sweet June morning, and watched and listened. ... When a shell came crashing through the trees near the house, [it] reminded us that we were in danger."

A surgeon came to the McDonald house carrying a wounded man. "Crowd after crowd of men continued to pour into the porch till it was packed full; then they crowded as close as they could get to be sheltered by the angle of the house."

An increased number of battles brought higher death tolls. The families of the dead rarely got to bury their loved ones. Instead, they placed markers where graves might have been. "Eliza and Emma went over to the graveyard and put up a white cross with John's name on it and the date of the Battle of Seven Pines," wrote Virginian Lucy Breckenridge. "It is only a temporary mark for the grave. All of his brothers and sisters wish to raise a monument to his memory, the first of our band who has been taken from us."

PERSONAL SACRIFICES

During the long war, Southern women ran households, raised children, and did endless chores. They went to church on Sunday and read Bibles in their parlors. They passed lonely evenings sewing, mending, or knitting socks

Southern women sewed uniforms for the Confederate soldiers.

for soldiers. "Let us work for them with our needles as long as they defend us with their bayonets," said Maria Louisa Fleet, who ran her family's plantation.

Growing crops and running businesses became difficult as men left to join the fighting. Most women who ran plantations had a very hard time. They had difficulty managing their large slave populations, which was a job

For many Southern women, the Civil War years were filled with suffering.

they did not want. Cotton production dropped by 3 million bales from 1861 to 1862. Many plantations failed, and women, once living in luxury, became homeless or took on whatever work they could to make ends meet. Some slave women lost their homes, too, since their owners could not afford to keep them. With no money and limited opportunities, these women struggled to survive. Most often, plantation mistress and slave banded together to feed and tend the children and keep the household from ruin.

Many African-American slave women knew how to live off the land. They taught their mistresses how to cook turnip, collard, and mustard greens, as well as hominy grits and fat back. These foods, which had been included in most Southerners' diets for some time, also became staples in elite Southern womens' diets during the hard times following the war. African-American women also knew how to heal using herbs and folk remedies. With most medicine going to the war effort, these folk remedies were essential for curing the sick.

Former slave women found themselves in even more peculiar situations. Amid all the turmoil and hardships, enslaved people in the South were declared free in 1863 with President Abraham Lincoln's Emancipation Proclamation. However, there was a difference between being declared free by the federal government and actually being free. Many slaves did not realize they were free, and many slave owners did not let slaves go. Slaves had no money, no homes, no property, and no place to go. Most could not read or write because they had not been allowed to learn. Where could a "free" slave go? Although it seems an odd choice today, many African-Americans stayed with their former owners. In times of war, a warm bed, food, and a roof overhead might seem better than going off alone.

As the war progressed, Confederate money lost value. Stores had almost nothing for sale because the Union blockade stopped most shipping into the South. Women depended on shops for everyday goods, such as needles, yarn, sugar, flour, salt, and spices, but slowly, store shelves

The Emancipation Proclamation went into effect on January 1, 1863.

A $100 note issued by the Confederate States of America

grew empty. The price of what was left was ridiculously high. Floride Clemson of South Carolina, wrote, "Just to think that sugar is about $20 a lb! Salt is at *least* 300$ a bushel of 50 lbs." Today, salt sells for about 70 cents a pound and sugar costs about 50 cents a pound.

As the war continued, women faced new threats. Union and Confederate looters stole horses, mules, wagons, clothing, jewelry, and anything else they could find. Women were forced to hide their livestock in the woods and bury casks of salt under piles of ashes. One Virginia woman tried to save her sterling silver from raiding

A Richmond, Virginia, street was in ruins.

Northerners. She sewed her silverware into her skirts.
When an officer came to inspect her house, she ushered
him up the stairs. To her embarrassment, her hems gave

way and showered silver utensils all over. The polite Union officer kindly picked up the forks and spoons and returned them to the woman.

Not every situation proved quite so friendly. Many women were beaten, robbed, and left with nothing. Troops camped in people's front yards while their horses grazed on the crops. Wounded soldiers slept in parlors and shared what little food remained.

As early Confederate victories gave way to defeats, women became more and more discouraged. They wanted their husbands and sons to come home—no matter what. But they did not give up. Southerner Sarah Morgan wrote in her diary, "I would want to fight until we win the cause so many have died for ... I want the South to conquer, dictate its own terms, and [then] go back to the Union." Hopes and dreams were all that Southern women had left.

Then, the Yankees came.

THE YANKEES ARE COMING!

Starting in 1864, Union General William T. Sherman and 62,000 troops swept through Georgia on their way to the Carolinas. They battled for territory against war-weary Confederate troops. Women in Virginia and Mississippi had grown used to having the Yankees camped on their doorsteps. The Union had come to those states fairly early in the war. However,

Union General William Tecumseh Sherman

women in Georgia and the Carolinas found themselves in unfamiliar circumstances as the Yankees advanced.

Before the war, Rebecca Felton lived a comfortable, wealthy lifestyle in Georgia. By 1864, she'd lost her

General Sherman's troops marched through Georgia and into South Carolina.

home and moved into a shack. That fall, dreadful news
came her way: Sherman and his troops were on the march.
The Yankees were coming. Many women and children fled
the oncoming Army. Not Rebecca Felton. "I can run no

further—I have nowhere to go," she said.

Said Georgian Ella Mitchell, "the road was a mass of blue men, the surrounding fields were full of them. In a few minutes our house was filled with the surging mass. In a little while there was not a piece of china, silver, or even the table cloth left, and the food disappeared in a second. ... Then the jail, the court house, peoples' barns and a large factory that made buckets and saddletrees, were all ablaze." Southern women called the land burnt country, after the ash-covered fields left behind.

In November 1864, Sherman's soldiers set fire to Atlanta and began their famous March to the Sea. Union troops met almost no resistance, but when they did, they destroyed everything in sight. Sherman believed in leaving nothing behind that Southerners could use to stop the Union forces.

By Christmas, Sherman's troops had marched across Georgia and taken Savannah. Then, it was northward into South Carolina. The women there trembled with fear over

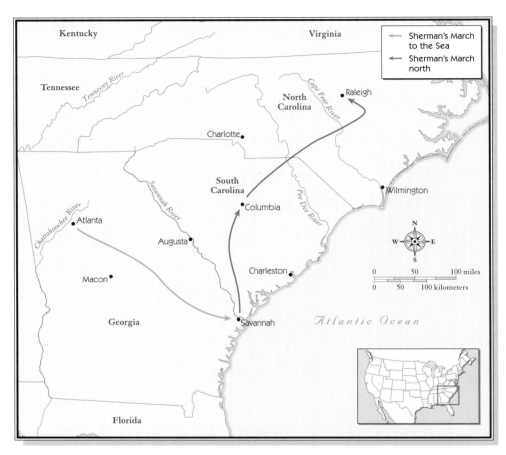

Sherman's troops marched from Atlanta to Savannah, Georgia. Then they went north to Columbia, South Carolina, and Raleigh, North Carolina.

Sherman's approach. They heard rumors that the Yankees would punish South Carolina for being the first state to leave the Union and enter the war. Government officials packed their bags and fled. The women had no place to go. Most remained, resigned to suffer whatever Sherman handed out.

Within days, Columbia burned. Red-gold flames lit the night sky, rising in every direction. While Sherman's troops have long been blamed for the fire, historians now

Columbia, South Carolina, was almost destroyed by fire.

In their sweep through Georgia, General Sherman's troops ripped apart railroads.

believe retreating Confederate soldiers started the fire so
that the cotton crops wouldn't fall into the hands of the
Yankees. The fire destroyed much of Columbia, leaving
its citizens homeless and defeated. Sherman's destructive
march, along with the successes of other Union generals,
ended any hopes that the South could win the Civil War.

THE PRICE OF PEACE

By April 1865, the South lay in ruins. Union soldiers had cut telegraph wires and bombed bridges. Train tracks lay in heaps of tangled iron. Roads were in such bad shape that travel became nearly impossible. News trickled down from city to town, and for Southern women, the news was nearly all bad.

By 1865, much of Charleston, South Carolina, had been destroyed.

Lee (right) surrendered to Grant in the home of Wilmer and Virginia McLean.

On April 2, 1865, Confederate government officials deserted Richmond. Four days later, Confederate General Robert E. Lee surrendered to Union General Ulysses S. Grant at Appomattox Court House, Virginia.

Once more, the women were left to deal with the invading Army. On the streets, Union blue uniforms replaced Confederate gray. For the women who ran

hospitals, supplies dried up. They had to beg Union officials for medicine, food, and bandages for wounded soldiers.

As the Yankees moved in, Confederate troops ran
away, burned buildings, and robbed their own people.
South Carolinian Pauline DeCaradeuc Heyward wrote,
"There is no use in trying to delude myself any longer, our
men have behaved disgracefully, have deserted, straggled,
& everything else. ... The Yankees are undisputed masters
of this betrayed land, and their iron heel is already pressed
upon the conquered."

If the Yankees seemed cruel that first week of April,
the weeks to come brought even worse actions. President
Abraham Lincoln was felled by an assassin's bullet on
April 14, 1865. He died the next day. Many Northerners
wanted to punish the South for the actions of Southern
assassin John Wilkes Booth. But the South was already
being punished.

The Civil War casualty list recorded more than
260,000 Southern soldiers dead. Nearly every woman lost

John Wilkes Booth shot President Lincoln at Ford's Theatre in Washington, D.C.

a father, brother, husband, or son. After the war ended, women mourned their dead. "We marched through the three grave yards, Baptist, Methodist, & Episcopal, wreathing each soldier's grave as we came to it, with wreaths we wore over our shoulders," recalled Floride Clemson.

The Confederate cause died. Banks closed, leaving

After the war, Southern women were left mourning the thousands of dead soldiers.

people holding worthless Confederate dollars and savings bonds. Thousands of homes and millions of bales of cotton and tobacco lay in ashes. The defeated soldiers came home—injured, hungry, and barefoot. Southern women could do one thing—hold their heads high and survive.

GLOSSARY

abolitionists—people who supported the banning of slavery

assassinated—murdered, often for political reasons

blockade—the use of warships to shut down trade or communication with a port or ports

commissioned—given a military rank

Confederate—a supporter of the Confederate States of America

house arrest—confinement, often under guard, to one's home instead of in prison

perseverance—the ability to persist in an undertaking despite discouragement

seceded—withdrew from a group

Union—the United States of America; also the Northern states that fought against the Southern states in the Civil War

Yankees—people who fought for the Union during the Civil War

DID YOU KNOW?

- Captain Sally Louisa Tompkins, the nurse who ran Robertson House hospital, was the only commissioned female captain in the Confederate Army.

- In 1865, Belle Boyd wrote *Belle Boyd in Camp and Prison*, a book about her adventures as a spy and soldier for the Confederacy.

- Laura Ratcliffe of Virginia allowed the Confederate Army to use her home as a headquarters. She also acquired information and money for John Singleton Mosby and his rangers. She hid the items under a large rock near her home, where Mosby would eventually pick them up.

- Mary Breckenridge, wife of Confederate Secretary of War John C. Breckenridge, once sewed a flag out of one of her silk dresses. The flag, presented to the 20th Tennessee Regiment, survived many battles.

IMPORTANT DATES

Timeline

1860	In November, Abraham Lincoln is elected president of the United States; in December, South Carolina secedes from the Union.
1861	In April, Confederate troops attack Fort Sumter, and the Civil War begins; in September, Sally Louisa Tompkins is appointed captain of the Confederate Army.
1862	Phoebe Pember becomes matron of Chimborazo, a military hospital in Richmond, Virginia.
1863	In January, the Emancipation Proclamation goes into effect; that summer, Belle Boyd is taken to Carroll Prison.
1864	Union General William T. Sherman destroys Atlanta, and his troops begin their March to the Sea.
1865	In April, Confederate General Robert E. Lee surrenders to Union General Ulysses S. Grant; Abraham Lincoln is assassinated.

IMPORTANT PEOPLE

BELLE BOYD (1843–1900)
Confederate spy from Martinsburg, Virginia (now West Virginia), who was arrested at least six times

MARY CHESNUT (1823–1886)
A Southern diarist whose book A Diary from Dixie *documents many important events, such as the attack on Fort Sumter, and gives insight into Confederate women's lives*

ROSE O'NEAL GREENHOW (1817–1864)
Confederate spy eventually discovered and placed under house arrest by the Union Army and then sent to live in the South; she drowned at sea

PHOEBE PEMBER (1823–1913)
Civil War nurse who became matron of Chimborazo military hospital in Richmond, Virginia; she wrote about her experiences in A Southern Woman's Story

SALLY LOUISA TOMPKINS (1833–1916)
A commissioned captain in the Confederate Army and a nurse

WANT TO KNOW MORE?

At the Library

Caravantes, Peggy. *Petticoat Spies: Six Women Spies of the Civil War*.
Greensboro, N.C.: Morgan Reynolds, 2002.

Chang, Ina. *A Separate Battle: Women and the Civil War*. New York: Puffin
Books, 1996.

Currie, Stephen. *Women of the Civil War*. San Diego: Lucent Books, 2003.

Schomp, Virginia. *The Civil War*. New York: Benchmark Books, 2004.

Zeinert, Karen. *Those Courageous Women of the Civil War*. Brookfield,
Conn.: Millbrook Press, 1998.

On the Web

For more information on *Women of the Confederacy*, use FactHound
to track down Web sites related to this book.

1. Go to *www.facthound.com*

2. Type in a search word related to this book
   or this book ID: 0756520339

3. Click on the *Fetch It* button.

Your trusty FactHound will fetch the best Web sites for you!

On the Road

The Museum of the Confederacy

1201 E. Clay St.

Richmond, VA 23219

804/649-1861

Historic documents and
artifacts from the Confederate
States of America

The National Civil War Museum

One Lincoln Circle at

Reservoir Park

Harrisburg, PA 17105-1861

717/260-1861

Artifacts, documents, and photographs from the Union and
Confederate sides of the Civil War

Look for more We the People books about this era:

The Assassination of Abraham Lincoln
ISBN 0-7565-0678-6

Battle of the Ironclads
ISBN 0-7565-1628-5

The Carpetbaggers
ISBN 0-7565-0834-7

The Confederate Soldier
ISBN 0-7565-2025-8

The Dred Scott Decision
ISBN 0-7565-2026-6

The Emancipation Proclamation
ISBN 0-7565-0209-8

Fort Sumter
ISBN 0-7565-1629-3

The Gettysburg Address
ISBN 0-7565-1271-9

Great Women of the Civil War
ISBN 0-7565-0839-8

The Lincoln-Douglas Debates
ISBN 0-7565-1632-3

The Missouri Compromise
ISBN 0-7565-1634-X

The Reconstruction Amendments
ISBN 0-7565-1636-6

Surrender at Appomattox
ISBN 0-7565-1626-9

The Underground Railroad
ISBN 0-7565-0102-4

The Union Soldier
ISBN 0-7565-2030-4

Women of the Union
ISBN 0-7565-2035-5

A complete list of We the People titles is available on our Web site:
www.compasspointbooks.com

INDEX

About the Author

Barbara A. Somervill has been writing for more than 30 years. She has written newspaper and magazine articles, video scripts, and books for children. She enjoys writing about history, science, and investigating people's lives for biographies. Ms. Somervill lives with her husband in South Carolina.